Ellen on the 2002 *Atlantis* space shuttle mission

Each day **Mission Control** on Earth wakes the astronauts by playing a song on the shuttle's radio. Today's song is played by the school band from the college Ellen Ochoa attended.

This is Ellen's fourth space mission, but her journey into space began when she was just a young girl with stars in her eyes.

Ellen was born on May 10, 1958, in Los Angeles, California. Her father's parents were born in Mexico. Ellen grew up with three brothers and a sister in La Mesa, California. As a young girl she was shy, quiet, and very intelligent. Ellen enjoyed school and loved to learn.

Ellen grew up in La Mesa, California, near San Diego.

Ellen Ochoa
Reaching for the Stars

By Vivian M. Cuesta

Contents

CELEBRATION PRESS
Pearson Learning Group

Stars in her Eyes

It is early morning. The sounds of a marching band fill the air inside the *Atlantis* **space shuttle**. Ellen Ochoa and the rest of the crew open their eyes. It is April 11, 2002. The **astronauts** are about to start the third day of their mission in space, working at the International Space Station.

Ellen Ochoa is the first Latina astronaut in space.

Apollo 11 commander Neil Armstrong and astronaut Edwin E. Aldrin during the first moon landing in 1969

In the fifth grade Ellen wanted to become President of the United States. That year, Neil Armstrong became the first person to set foot on the Moon. Back then, Ellen never imagined that one day she would make history in space, too.

Preparing for Takeoff

Ellen graduated from high school in 1975 and started college at nearby San Diego State University.

At first Ellen wanted to study either business or music. After taking some math classes, she became interested in studying science.

Ellen graduated first in her class from San Diego State University in 1980. That same year Ellen went to Stanford University to continue studying science in the graduate school. She earned two advanced degrees and became an engineer.

Ellen was still in graduate school in 1983 when Sally Ride became the first American female astronaut. Sally Ride inspired many women like Ellen to consider a career in space.

Sally Ride opened the door for future female astronauts.

In 1985 Ellen applied to NASA (National Aeronautics and Space Administration). She hoped to become an astronaut. She was interviewed for the job two years later, but was not chosen.

Even though Ellen was not accepted into the astronaut training program the first time, she did not give up her dream. Ellen still hoped to become an astronaut.

In the meantime, Ellen kept on working as an engineer. She did research at Sandia National Laboratories and also at NASA Ames Research Center in California.

Ellen and other engineers worked together to invent three special computer **systems**. One helps a computer identify objects in an image. One can help find certain types of problems in manufactured equipment. Another makes computerized pictures clearer and easier to study.

These systems had many uses in space exploration. In a way, her work as an engineer and researcher helped prepare Ellen to explore space herself one day.

Blast Off!

In 1990 NASA interviewed Ellen again. NASA was very impressed by her work as an engineer and researcher. This time Ellen was chosen to be an astronaut!

Ellen began NASA's astronaut training program. Most of the training taught her how to operate the space shuttle.

During her astronaut training, Ellen simulates a parachute jump.

Here is Ellen during her water survival training.

Ellen also learned how to operate a robotic arm, and fly jet airplanes.

In July 1991, Ellen completed the training program and became a NASA astronaut. She was the first **Latina** astronaut in history!

Now Ellen practiced what she had learned about the space shuttle using a **simulator**. She also learned what **weightlessness** feels like. In space, astronauts experience weightlessness because of the speed and direction that the space shuttle is traveling. The astronauts get an introduction to weightlessness by flying on a special plane called the "Vomit Comet." It makes climbs and steep dives like a roller coaster.

Ellen also learned how to test equipment. She learned what to do in case of an emergency on the space shuttle. As a result of their training, Ellen and her fellow astronauts knew they could handle any problems in space.

Ellen trained for almost three years before her first mission into space. Finally, in April 1993, she flew on the *Discovery* space shuttle.

Ellen is a mission specialist. That means she is often in charge of the scientific experiments on a space mission. Her first mission lasted nine days. She did experiments to study the effect of the Sun on Earth's atmosphere.

Ellen with the crew of her 1994 mission to space

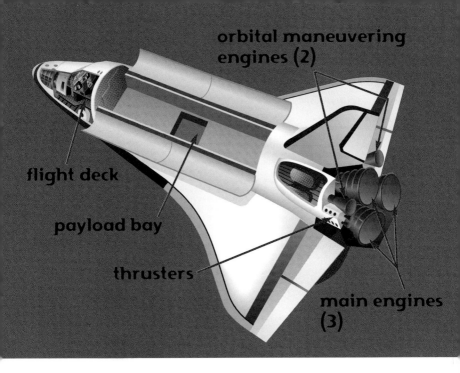

This cutaway drawing shows some of the space shuttle's parts.

Ellen's second space mission was in November 1994. On this trip she did more solar energy experiments.

When she is in space, Ellen uses her skills as an engineer and also her leadership skills. An astronaut must be able to work well with other people.

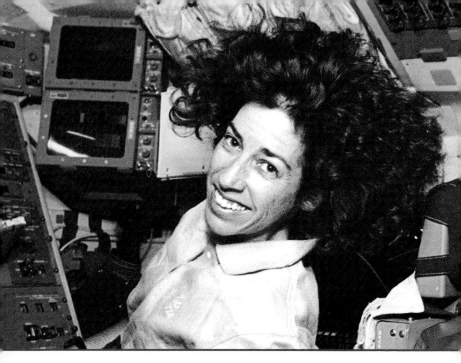

Look how Ellen's hair stands up because of weightlessness!

On all of her missions, Ellen worked a **robotic arm**. She used it to catch objects in space, like satellites, or to move space-walking crew members around.

In April 2002, Ellen operated the new International Space Station robotic arm. She used it to help attach and activate a new piece of equipment for the station.

Out of This World

Have you ever wondered what Earth looks like from a space shuttle? "It is a very beautiful sight," Ellen says. "You can see cities, mountain ranges, lakes. We never got tired of looking at it."

Many students ask Ellen what it is like to live onboard a space shuttle. While on a mission, astronauts mostly eat freeze-dried food. One of Ellen's favorite foods to eat in space is tortillas. Astronauts like them because, unlike bread, they don't leave crumbs floating in the spacecraft. Floating crumbs are hard to clean up.

On her first two trips into space Ellen slept in a sleep unit that looked like a long box. On her third mission she slept in a sleeping bag attached to the wall with hooks. The astronauts even use a special toilet on the space shuttle.

Ellen is the first flutist to play in space!

Astronauts must get used to many things that are different from life on Earth. They keep in touch with their lives back at home, though. When Ellen is in space, she uses e-mail to send messages to her family. To relax, Ellen sometimes even likes to play her flute on the shuttle!

Back on Earth

When she is not in space on a mission, Ellen works at the Lyndon B. Johnson Space Center in Houston, Texas. She does research, tests equipment and software, and helps develop procedures and training programs. Ellen has also worked in Mission Control, where she talks with other astronauts in space to assist them with their mission.

In Mission Control, Ellen helps astronauts in space talk with NASA on Earth.

Ellen has received seven awards from NASA for her work. These include the Outstanding Leadership medal in 1995 and the Exceptional Service Medal in 1997.

Part of her job is to speak to students about being an astronaut and about the importance of education. "Education is what allows you to stand out," she says.

Ellen and the people at NASA work together to explore space.

Speaking to students about space is very important to Ellen.

Ellen encourages students to be excited about math and science. Her strong math and science skills have allowed her to have an interesting and challenging career. She is an engineer, an inventor, and an astronaut.

Ellen's family thinks she is out of this world!

Ellen is also a wife and mom. She is married to Coe Fulmer Miles. They have two children. She enjoys playing volleyball and biking. She has a license to fly small planes. She plays the flute and was a member of an orchestra when she was a student.

Reaching for the Stars

One of Ellen's most important jobs is being a **role model**. Her own role model was her mother, Rosanne Ochoa. She taught Ellen and her brothers and sister the importance of hard work and getting a good education. Today Ellen teaches the same lessons to young people who dream of becoming an astronaut.

Ellen Ochoa is a role model for many people.

Ellen at work. Notice the tortilla near her right hand.

Ellen is a role model for many people because she didn't just dream about reaching the stars. She dared to make her dream come true. "Don't be afraid to reach for the stars," she says. "I believe a good education can take you anywhere on Earth and beyond."

IMPORTANT EVENTS IN SPACE HISTORY

January 31, 1958:
The first U.S. satellite, *Explorer I*, is sent into space.

February 20, 1962:
John Glenn, Jr., becomes the first American to orbit Earth.

June 18, 1983:
Sally Ride becomes the first American woman in space.

September 12, 1992:
Mae C. Jemison becomes the first African American woman in space.

November 20, 1998:
The first part of the International Space Station is launched.

1955

1965

1975

1985

1995

2005

May 5, 1961:
Alan B. Shepard Jr. becomes the first American in space.

July 20, 1969:
During the *Apollo 11* mission, Neil Armstrong becomes the first person to walk on the Moon.

August 30, 1983:
Guion S. Bluford Jr. becomes the first African American in space.

April 8, 1993:
Ellen Ochoa becomes the first Latina astronaut in space.

July 23, 1999:
Astronaut Eileen Collins becomes the first female commander of a space shuttle.

23

Glossary

astronaut	a person trained to travel in space
Latina	a woman of Latin American origin living in the United States
Mission Control	the NASA engineers who work on the ground during a space mission
robotic arm	a mechanical arm guided by controls
role model	a person who serves as an example to others
simulator	a machine that helps someone practice something by pretending
space shuttle	a spacecraft designed to carry people and equipment between Earth and space
system	a set of tools that work together
weightlessness	the state of having little or no weight